The Adventures of Sheila and Gaston The Cat

Sheila Tanguy Tracey

Copyright © 2025 by Sheila Tanguy Tracey

All rights reserved. No part of this publication may be reproduced, distributed, or transmitted in any form or by any means, including photocopying, recording, or other electronic or mechanical methods, without the prior written permission of the author, except in the case of brief quotations embodied in critical reviews and certain other noncommercial uses permitted by copyright law.

978-1-965552-47-6 (Hardback)
Library of Congress Control Number 2025920697

admin@bookwrightshouse.com
☎ (213) 286 6700

Sheila was from Morristown, a small town in New Jersey. The Traceys had a house in the countryside and two cats who were sisters and a German Shepherd & Colie mix dog. A letter came in the mail addressed to her father and mother. It said," the County of Morristown was going to build a highway where our house was located and we must relocate immediately". We gave the two cats and dog to another family in the area who had a farm. Then packed our car. Sheila did not want to leave Morristown.

It was the Fall season and the Tracey Family just sold their house in New Jersey and the father drove for 3 and a half days to California, on the Pacific Coast with winter approaching. It was a few months now since they arrived in San Francisco. Sheila was six years old and it was winter break. Both Sheila and her brother were enrolled in Argon Elementary School, in the Richmond District. Both Sheila and her brother missed their pets. Winter was boring and their parents promised a cat for the new house if they were good. Winter in San Francisco was mild in comparison to the sleet, snow and ice that they were used to in New Jersey. Argon was within walking distance from the new home. It was Saturday, when their mother announced that Brendan and Sheila could go with her to the San Francisco SPCA and look for a suitable cat to adopt.

They went to the SPCA and found that there were an abondance of pets to choose from. Mother found a cage with Orange and White striped Tabby Kittens in it. There were only two Tabby kittens left in that cage.

Little did Mother know that these were not ordinary kittens; they could talk and understand Brendan and Sheila. The care taker opened the cage and before doing so, Mother asked if we could see the male kitten. The other one was a female. They were both two weeks old. Mother held the male kitten in her arms. Gee wiz, the male kitten meowed. It's so nice to be out of this cage. Whops, I think your leaving my sister behind. Mother, this kitten can talk, said Sheila. Can we take him home with us? So, mother decided to go ahead and sign the adoption papers for this cat. The Tracey family brought him home. After dinner, the parents asked the children if they had any ideas for a name for the new kitten. Finally, it was Mother's turn. She thought of a French name for him, Gaston. It was a winner and she gave the kitten the name, Gaston. It was a common French name from the mid 1900's.

The Adventures of Sheila and Gaston The Cat

It was 1962, Sheila's older brother Brendan was enrolled in Argon Elementary school which was four blocks away from our house. They loved their little cat and kept him at home until he was old enough to go outside. In the meanwhile, Mother bought some Purina Kitten food and some milk for Gaston. She also bought some cat litter and put it in a box in the family room. Gee whiz! Exclaimed Gaston, "The food was better than in the shelter." Gaston meowed to Brendan and Sheila. Three years went by and the Tracey family moved from the Richmond District to the Noe Valley District in San Francisco. This time the house was larger and Gaston entertained himself by catching mice in the strawberry patch at the other end of the large backyard. Bonne Appetite, just like a real San Francisco, French Cat that he was. There were also plenty of snails. Rumor has it that, a Frenchman dropped a bag of French snails in his yard, in San Francisco and thus the snail population grew in every yard in San Francisco. You can't eat them because people spray pesticides on the snails and they could be harmful to eat. Gaston was not a fussy eater he also loved his Purina cat food with a bowl of fresh milk.

He was a happy camper with both Brendan and Sheila to play with in the house. One day when Sheila was ten and a half years old; all of us packed our belongs into our VW Bug car. "Golly Gee, it looks like we are going on a trip, am I invited? meowed Gaston, to Brendan and Sheila. You are coming too, said the children. They left San Francisco, to go to the mountainous region of Mexico. Father drove them all the way with Gaston on his lap. Then Sheila took turns with Gaston, on her father's lap. then Mother held Gaston, in her arms, on her lap. Then it was Brendan's turn to take the cat while mother held the map in her hand, giving Father directions. She also held a thermos, and poured cups of hot tea for everyone. She also had a picknick basket at her feet filled with tuna fish, peanut and jelly sandwiches. She also had apple slices and orange slices in zip lock bags, in the basket. She kept the tea cups in the glove compartment. Gaston would drink powdered milk in a cup and he ate Purina cat food out of the can. Brendan and Sheila slept in the back seat of the car.

Father drove all the way to Mid Western Texas and entered Mexico through the border town of El Paso. They stopped at the local bank and exchanged dollars for pesos in El Paso. Mother went to the supermarket to buy some food and hot coffee. All of them got back in the car and Father drove until he ran out of gas in Guadalajara. They went to a full serve gas station in the city and father paid exact change for the gas and they left the city. He drove all night long in the mountains until dusk. The sun rose in the east, it was beautiful. They arrived in Leon, it was early evening. They stopped at a local café and ate a light dinner. They got gas at a service station and they left Leon. Brendan and Sheila got Gaston to come to the backseat with them and he stayed there all the way to San Miguel de Allende. This mountain town was just a hundred miles north of Mexico City. Arriva! Arriva Mexico ... They reached their destination! It was dusk and their father bought the local newspaper and found an apartment for rent in town. They were lucky. After unpacking a few blankets, clothes and food that was still in the car and putting them in their new apartment, they ventured to see the activities in the town square.

There was a group of fiancés, newly weds and singles marching in their Sunday best clothes, walking in procession around the town square on the weekends. Vendors sold desserts and Fanta sodas in front of the stores there. Brendan and Sheila took Gaston for his nightly walk on a leash after, coming back from the town square. That morning Mother went to the church in the town square, to ask the priest where the local catholic school was and the phone number. Mother and Father took Brendan and Sheila to San Domingo School on the outskirts of town. We were enrolled and started school the next day. Mother placed an advertisement in the paper, to give private French and English Lessons. Mother and Father enrolled in Painting & Sculpture classes, at the Instituto des Artes and a few evening classes in Metal work at Las Bellas Artes, also in San Miguel de Allende. Gaston attended to his uncanny adventures in the city.

Sheila Tanguy Tracey

Along the streets leading to the town square were shops where one could purchase vegetables, fruits, meat, tortillas, tamales, clothes, shoes, bread, pastries and gifts in the open market and shops. The apartment complex was within walking distance to Santa Domingo Catholic School and in the opposite direction, to the center of town. Brendan and Sheila had to wear school uniforms. Gaston no longer went for walks at night, on his leash. He was free to roam the neighborhood on his own accord. There was no such thing as cat food at the Super Mercado. Mother had to buy ½ a kilo ground beef for him every day. The fisty cat ate with subtle vigor ¼ of a kilo of meat twice a day. Gaston loved it so much he would purr the entire time he feasted. Mother would also buy groceries for the rest of the family and cook three meals a day.

Eggs, milk and cereal for breakfast. Soups, salads and sandwiches for lunch. Meat, fish, potatoes and rice for dinner. Gaston, Sheila, Brendan, Mother and Father left San Miguel de Allende, together. This time they rented a villa in a silver mining town in the mountains near Leon. They called Marfil their home for three months. Brendan and Sheila were enrolled in a Catholic school just up the creek behind the house. Gaston didn't like scorpions, but he did eat the bugs. There were plenty of them in the house. Both Mother and Father worked as English and French teachers. When they came home, they taught both Brendan and Sheila Spanish and French grammar before dinner time.

Brendan and Sheila played beyond the creek, behind the house with the other children in the neighborhood. Girls wore long pants or jeans under their dresses. Boys and girls had sling shots made of wood and a strong rubber band. They used these with stones to fling at birds in the trees. Sheila wanted to play one Saturday morning and Brendan had already left with some friends. She exited outside her veranda, over the wall and onto the tree branch which reached over the creek. A boy leading a donkey, carrying wood was on the other side of the water. Sheila wanted to practice her Spanish and make a new friend. She quickly jumped down from the tree branch and introduced herself.

Sheila Tanguy Tracey

Sheila asked him if she could ride his donkey. He agreed and he helped her up on to the donkey's back. She rode all the way to his house where she got off and said," she missed her parents and brother". He did not understand and offered her some milk and fruit. It was getting late and the sun was setting. She said," where are my parents?" So, a loud knock and a man's voice came through the front door, it was Father! She came running into his arms. Yes, Father found her. He was angry but happy to see his daughter was safe and took her home immediately. Brendan was at home with Mother and Gaston. Yes, Sheila could no longer play outside with their friends and could only spend her time painting and drawing afterschool and on weekends. Inside the house were a nest of Scorpions. Gaston used to hiss at them when they came too close to him. The Tracey's used to leave their shoes on the front porch by the door. One afternoon, when the whole family was leaving home to go run errands in town. Every one was shaking their shoes before putting them on.

They were checking for Scorpions and other bugs. Mother turned her shoes upside down and shook them. Out of her shoe came a scorpion ready for an attack with its tail high in the air. Mother was horrified and accused Father of putting the scorpion in her shoe. Father was bewildered and said nothing. They went to Leon for lunch while Gaston stayed at home. It was time to move on and go back to San Miguel de Allende, it was Christmas. This time, they rented a house on the outskirts of town. Both Brendan and Sheila returned to Santa Domingo Catholic School. Their parents enrolled in classes at The Instituto des Artes and The Bellas Artes School both in downtown San Miguel de Allende.

Gaston didn't like being couped up in the house and went out. The journey unfolds as he didn't come home, still after ten days past and no sign of Gaston could be found. Mother took several pieces of paper, hammer, nails and a pen. She wrote on the papers and nailed the signs on to telephone poles and utility poles throughout the city limits. The signs read: We are a sad family whose Children are crying and want our tiger stripped cat back. We will give a handsome reward. Then She put it down on the flyer.

Sheila Tanguy Tracey

Twelve days had past and no sign of Gaston, however late in the afternoon there was a mature Mexican Lady who knocked constantly at the door. She had a large shawl on and leading to its' opening in the front was a long rope which she held onto. She asked Mother if she was missing a cat and if there was a reward. Mother asked her if they could see this cat she found. She said she found the cat in the ravine near her house and saw the signs which indicated a reward. She proceeded to open her shawl and out came a skinny cat, almost hairless onto the threshold of the door. Mother immediately recognized Gaston and paid a handsome sum of 350.00 pesos to the lady, she left. Gaston couldn't even meow but he was glad to be home. Mother went to the butcher to buy meat and some milk at the Super mercado for Gaston. It took a month and a half before Gaston regained his health. They kept him indoors, taking turns to walk him on his leash outside. Their priority was his safety and recovery.

Winter was almost over and before classes started again; they made plans to move on. Only one thing the car was stolen. Father went to the local police department to file a report for the missing car. After a few days a carcass of a VW Bug car was found and there were no suspects. The police did not know who the thieves were and the missing parts of the car could not be found. Father went to see a local mechanic who said he could order the parts; wheels, tires, windshield wipers, engine belt, etc. So, time went by and it seemed as though Father was rebuying these parts that were stolen, from the mechanic's shop. There was nothing he could do. So, he went along with it. Finally, the car was ready and the Tracey Family was ready to leave San Miguel de Allende. This time they left Mexico and went to Canada. They packed the car and Gaston rode in the back seat all the way to Montreal, Quebec, Canada. We were arriving in Montreal, in time to see the opening of EXPO '1967, in January. Gaston said, "Gee whiz, now I am a true transcontinental cat."

It was snowing and cold in Montreal. Mother and Father purchased tickets for the entire family to ride on The Holland Liner. A Dutch American commercial passenger ship. The Tracey's had a few days before they embarked on their seaward journey to Le Havre, France. Those few days before they left, they explored Montreal and Expo 1967. They boarded The Rotterdam, one in the fleet of Holland Liner passenger ships. Gaston, stayed in the haul of the ship with all of the other animals on board. Father also made arrangements to take the car with them. The voyage took ten days. After two days at sea, everyone got seasick. They spent two days in their cabin getting over it. They ate their meals in the dining room and spent time on the deck of the ship. After lunch one day, there was an announcement of a children's talent show coming up. There would be a Beauty Contest, and Artist Contest and a Talent Contest for the children, on the sixth day of voyage. Both Brendan and Sheila entered a painting each. Sheila entered the Beauty Contest and Talent Contest as well.

The day came and Mother dressed Sheila in a new dress and combed Sheila's shoulder length hair. She put ribbons in Sheila's hair as well. The Talent Show started after lunch at 1 pm. Sheila made her way to The Dining Room where The Children's Talent Show was to take place. Brendan, Mother and Father followed. Sheila waited for her name to be called for the Beauty Show. Her name was called and she was summoned to the stage with the other girls. Sheila won and was crowned Miss Tulip. With a real crown of Tulips and won a Dutch doll with a bouquet of artificial tulips and wooden shoes. The Talent Show was next and there were only two contestants: Sheila and a little boy. The little boy went first. He sang a song but was out of key and Sheila was next. She sang "My Bonnie Lives Over the Ocean" an Irish Song. There was a band also on stage. They accompanied Sheila as she sang. She won The Talent Show. There was one more contest, The Art Contest. Sheila's drawing won first place and Brendan's drawing won second place. Father left the Dining Room in astonishment. Mother stayed and escorted Brendan and Sheila back to the cabin quietly. The Tracey children stole the show.

It was time to end their Atlantic Ocean journey and the Holland Liner was preparing to land at the port of Le Harvre, France within a couple of hours in the late afternoon. The Tracey family packed their bags once more and made their way off the ship. They were given back their cat and their car. Father pulled out a map of France and everyone got into the car including Gaston, who sat in the back seat of the VW Bug with Brendan and Sheila. Mother sat up front with Father at the wheel. He took the highway driving all the way to Paris. In Mexico, Brendan and Sheila's parents met Michel who had a family in Paris, France, Mother was originally from 15eme, in Paris, France. We went to the Left Bank district, near Saint Germain de Pres. 4 rue de Seine to be precise, where Michel's grandmother lived. Michel's Grandmother welcomed the Tracey Family with open arms and set them up, in one of her studio apartments in the building. It was located at the top of the stairs on the left side. Mother went to the bank and exchanged some money so they could pay the rent and buy some groceries. This time there was some cat food for Gaston too. Brendan and Sheila put Gaston on a leash and found a small park to walk the cat while Father unpacked the car.

The studio was small and everyone slept on the floor after eating dinner. In the morning, Mother found a school close by for Brendan and Sheila. It was time for them to learn another language, French. Mother talked to the grandmother about looking for work. She had a big heart and put Mother to work in her art gallery showcasing the front of the building facing the street. She also employed Father, as a handyman and this included painting the interior walls of the building. After school, Brendan and Sheila played battleship with Simone, another grandchild. Gaston stayed in the studio most of the day. Father had a WWII buddy who was stationed in Stuttgart, Germany. Father was in the US Army with him. Father took the entire family to Germany to visit this guy. Gaston rode in the back seat with Brendan and Sheila the entire way. When they arrived at their destination, it was night time. The moon was full and it began to rain. Father's friend lived in a house and had some children too.

Sheila Tanguy Tracey

Some how there was an argument among the adults in the house and Father said it was time to leave. Once again Gaston and the Tracey family hit the road and Father drove like lightening on the highway back to Paris. Mother and Father wanted to try their luck securing a small house in the French countryside and finding work there. The family packed their VW Bug, Gaston hopped inside with Brendan and Sheila in the back seat. This time the adventure took them to Orlean, where Jeane D'arc was from, in the Loire valley. It was a small town and a farming community. Mother waisted no time in enrolling Brendan and Sheila in school. This time, it was a public school and the principal insisted that the Tracey children should be two years behind because of their lack of knowledge of the French language. Sheila made a friend in class and after school she ate Pain au Chocolat with her new friend. Brendan and Sheila played outside the house with their friends on weekends. Gaston stayed at home until it was springtime. Mother and Father still looked for work in the surrounding towns. Still no luck. The Tracey family went back to Rue de Seine, in Paris.

This time, there was a 2 bedroom apartment available in the building. Brendan and Sheila still took Gaston to the neighborhood park, on a leash. Mother worked in the gallery and Father was still painting the walls in the interior of the building. Brendan and Sheila did not return to school and played all day long in the theater, behind the gallery, in the building. Gaston was house bound and enjoyed good French cat food. This situation lasted another couple of weeks until the Tracey's decided to leave France. As much as Mother loved Paris, she also agreed They should give Montreal, Quebec in Canada, a try. They said "Good Bye" to Simone, and her grandmother. in Paris. Gaston and the children poured into the back seat of the car and off they went to Brittany, France. Mother had family in Locronan, Brittany where her grandparents were from. In the village square was a carpenter, name Jobe. He could make wooden shoes and just about anything out of wood. Mother bought a brooch for Sheila. It was a tiny bagpipe made out of silver. Mother and Father took the children to Quimper, to some cousins who were making Gateau Breton or Brittany Cake.

The Adventures of Sheila and Gaston The Cat

Before leaving Brittany, Mother visited her Aunt Emily Tanguy, her father's sister. She was a retired teacher and never married. She enjoyed seeing Mother's husband and children and cat. Within the next few days, Gaston and the Tracey family boarded small boat and crossed the Atlantic Ocean, heading to Quebec, Canada. They took their VW Bug with them. It was the month of December and the entire family was seasick throughout the duration of the voyage. Brendan and Sheila played chess and card games to keep busy during the daytime. They were the only children on board. The adults were unfriendly. Gaston was in the cargo compartment, in the haul of the ship. So was the car. They were ten days at sea and swore not to ever take a boat again. Flying would have been a better option. It was in the month of December in 1967 when they arrived in Quebec, Canada. They took Gaston and the car off the boat at the dock and left for Montreal so they could enjoy the last few days of Expo '67.

Gaston was a city cat from San Francisco and was delighted to be on his leash; walking through all the different pavilions and expositions from around the globe. Brendan and Sheila took turns holding Gaston's leash. They saw the Moroccan Pavilion last with Gaston and their parents. It was time to leave so they went to town to search for an apartment to rent in the city. It was snowing and there was ice and sleet on the roads and on the sidewalks too. Mother enrolled Brendan and Sheila in Bilingual School, that's right, French and English. Half the day the courses would be in French then the rest of the day it was in English. Both Mother and Father found work right away. In the meanwhile, Gaston roamed the neighborhood. He would come back to the apartment through the window, off the fire escape. He would love the smell of homemade Maple Fudge which Father would make every weekend, also on his days off from work. He would light the gas oven and leave its door open the help heat up the apartment.

Sheila Tanguy Tracey

Sheila recalls one afternoon, letting Gaston out of the apartment through kitchen window which led to the fire escape. Several hours went by and no sight of Gaston. It was late at night and there was a faint meow coming from the window, it was Gaston. Sheila opened the curtain then the window to let him in. His tail was nearly severed in two and was bleeding. Mother, Mother cried Sheila. She came in to see what was happening and came back. She wrapped Gaston in a warm blanket and said to Father, Lets take him to the veterinarian. So, Father quickly put his shoes on and grabbed his keys and they left. When they arrived at the pet hospital, the vet operated on Gaston's tail right away. He did everything possible to save the poor cat's tail. I was in the early morning hours when Mother and Father came back home with Gaston whose tail was all bandaged up. How did this happen? Apparently, a neighbor slammed down a window on this poor cat's tail. It took several weeks for Gaston's tail to heal. The Tracey family moved to Ottawa, Ontario just in time for the Canadian Bicentennial celebration.

They stayed there a few months then moved on to Hull, Quebec across the Saint Lawrence River. Gaston stayed indoors and never left the apartment. It was springtime, all the flowers were in bloom, the snow was melting and it rained less frequently. The entire family including Gaston were missing their home in San Francisco, California. So, once again, Mother and Father packed up the car with blankets, clothes, sandwiches and hot tea in a thermos. Gaston had his leash attached to his collar and he rode in the back seat with Brendan and Sheila in the VW bug. Sheila painted a bumper sticked for the car. "San Francisco or Bust". Father affixed it to the rear bumper of the car before they left Hull. All five were ready to throw in the towel and embark on their journeys end, back to their roots. Father started the car and headed westward driving all the way to Banff, Alberta, a midwestern town in Canada. They stopped at an Indian Reservation. Father purchased some moccasins for Sheila.

The Adventures of Sheila and Gaston The Cat

They were made of handcrafted leather and beadwork. Brendan wasn't as interested and settled for banners to mount on his bedroom walls. Mother bought a few beaded necklaces. Father started heading south towards the US border to North Dakota. Yes, they crossed the line onto US soil. Once they were in the states we headed to Billings, Montana. When the Tracey family arrived in town, they stopped in front of a few stores on the main street. Father parked the car. A tall middle age man with a long winter coat, approached the car. Mother rolled down the window and asked if the was a place in town where she could buy a cup of coffee and get some gas? He replied" We don't like your kind of folks around here". "Get out of this town before I call the cops". So, Mother rolled up her window and Father put the pedal to the metal and drove out of town. Father drove them to the next small town to go to the bank and grocery store so Mother could buy some cat food, bread, tuna fish, mayonnaise, jelly and peanut butter so she could make sandwiches in the car. She also bought bottled water and some tea bags.

Father drove for two days, all the way to Oregon on highway 1. San Francisco was one day away in the south along the Pacific Coastline. Gaston began to meow. They were almost home. Father continued to drive down the coast until he reached the border of California. He kept on driving further south until they reached the Golden Gate Bridge with the fog rolling inwards and the cool misty air and windy breeze. Yes, they were finally merging towards the end of their journey with Gaston, their "well -traveled" cat. So, he continued to drive in San Francisco, to Valley and Noe streets, in the Noe Valley District, where they called home. When they got there, the house was empty so Mother and father unpacked the car and left to buy some groceries and put gas in the car. In the meanwhile, Brendan and Sheila unpacked the cat food and gave Gaston his first meal in San Francisco in over a year. Then Brendan let Gaston outside in the back yard, so he could reclaim his old territory. Eat mice and snails like a good San Franciscan tabby cat.

Sheila Tanguy Tracey

It was the summer of 1967 and Sheila was eleven years old. Mother bought an easel, canvases and some oil paints. Both Brendan and Sheila read books about American Indians. Sheila started painting Native American Indians and Horses. She signed her Artist name which was Ona, a name she had taken from a book. Mother and Father painted landscapes of the plains and Mexico. Father painted a silhouette of Gaston's back, seated at dusk ... With many colors. Brendan painted Gaston too, laying in the garden. He exhibited it in The Children's Art Show at the DeYoung Museum, in the Golden Gate Park in 1968. Mother graduated from Pacific Dental School in San Francisco and later became a registered Dental Nurse. Father went back to work at the US Post Office and also as a File Clerk for Social Security Administration, in San Francisco. Brendan attended Lowell High School, near 19th avenue. His bicycle gang met at the Tracey house twice a week to play ping pong and eat popcorn all night long. Sometimes, both Mother and Sheila would make crepes for the boys as well. Sheila had a group of girl friends too.

Once for a class assignment at James Lick Junior High school, she and a classmate made a recording of a mob applauding the sentencing to death of Marie Antoinette during The French Revolution. Ken and Charlie, from next door helped by recording from a record of sound effects and recording a paper cutter in motion for the sound of the guillotine. Both Sheila and her classmate, Suzanne were both of French heritage but the teacher thought this was too controversial to share with the class. They were given a lower grade because of it even though the project was very realistic. Ken and Charlie opened their doors to both the girls and the boys after school hours. Gaston proved to us he was able to adapt to different surroundings and countries during his travels outside of San Francisco and readapt himself to the city life again. He was a true survivor of circumstances, different times and different environments.

It was 1972, Father had a car accident on Oak Street in San Francisco. He was giving a ride to Vanessa, a lady from his workplace. She broke her arm and Father had insurance. He gave his car away to a young couple who just had a baby and were going to South Dakota. Mother had an operation at Mont Zion Hospital. Father came to visit her and had kicked her bed. When she came out of the hospital, she called her lawyer to file for a divorce. She put Brendan and Sheila on an airplane going to Paris, France. A Year later, Sheila came back and Mother lived in the house alone with Gaston. Star took Mother and Sheila to Venture Lodge in Pescadero, California. She left Gaston with Rick at the lodge. Mother found work with Civil Service in Monterey. Sheila went back to San Francisco to live with Father in the house and graduated from Mission High School. Gaston learned to live in the wild.

Rick did not feed him but he kept Rick company on cold nights. There were trees, squirrels, raccoons, mice, foxes and other animals in the woods surrounding Venture Lodge. Gaston lived there until his 14th Birthday in 1976. Rick went for a walk one fine day in the woods and heard a noise or a thump. He thought he saw something, so he looked around and saw Gaston lying there on the ground beneath a tree. A cat usually lands on his feet but this time apparently, he was in a tree and had fell to his death. Rick phoned Mother and Sheila in Monterey. Gaston had reached his journey's end, he was well traveled cat. The adventures of Gaston had come to an end.

Bibliography

Illustrations done by Sheila Tanguy Tracey:

The Adventures of Sheila & Gaston, The Cat (Cover)

    1. Gaston in San Francisco, California 1962 p. 1

    2. Gaston in Marfil, Mexico 1966 p. 4

    3. San Miguel de Allende, Gaston in Mexico 1966 p. 5

    4. Gaston in Montreal, Canada 1967 P. 10

Solo Photograph of Sheila courtesy of boat, Rotterdam of Holland Lines 1967 p. 7

Photographs: courtesy of Brendan Tracey, family photo collection:

    1. Gaston the traveling Cat p. 8

    2. Gaston, Brendan & Sheila in Brittany, France 1967 p. 9

    3. Brendan & Sheila on the road, San Francisco or Bust 1967 p. 11

    4. Brendan, Gaston, Mother & Sheila Yoho National Park 1967 p. 12

Paintings by Joseph G. Tracey 1967 Oils on Canvas

1. San Miguel de Allende, Mexico p. 3
2. Gaston in the Mountains p. 13